The Realities of Life

My Innermost Thoughts

Lorna Ramirez

Published in Australia by Sid Harta Publishers Pty Ltd,
ABN: 46 119 415 842
23 Stirling Crescent, Glen Waverley, Victoria 3150 Australia
Telephone: +61 3 9560 9920, Facsimile: +61 3 9545 1742
E-mail: author@sidharta.com.au

First published in Australia June 2014
This edition published 2017
Copyright © Lorna Ramirez 2014
Cover design, typesetting: Chameleon Print Design

The right of Lorna Ramirez to be identified as the Author of the Work has been asserted in accordance with the Copyright, Designs and Patents Act 1988.

All rights reserved. No part of this publication may be reproduced, stored in a retrieval system, or transmitted, in any form or by any means without the prior written permission of the publisher, nor be otherwise circulated in any form of binding or cover other than that in which it is published and without a similar condition being imposed on the subsequent purchaser.

Ramirez, Lorna
The Realities of Life: My Innermost Thoughts
ISBN: 978-0-6482130-0-0
pp182

About the Author

Lorna Ramirez was born, raised and educated in Manila in the Philippines, attaining a degree in chemical engineering and working as a laboratory manager in a textiles company.

In 1977, with her husband and her son and daughter, she migrated to Australia. She worked as a laboratory technician and a chemist in Australia, only retiring in the year 2000 to care for her first grandchild.

Lorna Ramirez has travelled extensively, gaining much from her interactions with people all over the world and building a strong foundation for her philosophies about life. She loves gardening, cooking and reading and playing the piano. She is also interested in the stock exchange.

She has published two books: My Innermost Thoughts (now The Realities of Life) in 2014 and My Passion, My Calling in 2015. In October 2016 Lorna was one of the recipients of a certificate of recognition from FILCCA (Filipino Community Council of Australia).

Lorna is also a regular contributor for The Philippine Times in Melbourne and The Philippine Sentinel in Sydney. Throughout her life

Lorna Ramirez, a woman of faith, has been a wise observer of human behaviour and has collected her many wisdoms and observations to produce this inspiring and uplifting book.

Acknowledgements

My special thanks to
Marie Franze
Renalyn Cerezo

for helping me to make my dream of publishing a book of my own a reality.

To
My loving husband, Claro
My grandkids, Alyssa and Amelia
My children and their partners –
Carlo and Marie
Maritess and Steve

Preface

Any similarities to others' writings are coincidental. This is my original work.

My love and strong bonding with my family, my relationship with friends and extended family and my strong connection with God have inspired me.

I have explored my innermost feelings and offer my perspective on many aspects of life.

As I have matured my perceptions have changed because of my life's experiences and knowledge gained. I want to share the convictions and beliefs, value system and philosophies developed throughout my life.

My hope is that my innermost thoughts will touch and inspire you in some way.

Lorna Ramirez

My Poems

1. EACH TIME

Each time, we breathe to live
Each time, we should remember that life is a gamble
Each time is a challenge
Each time is a journey because no one knows what the future brings and holds
Yes, we can try to plan and control our lives
But much to our dismay, we soon discover we can only do it to a certain degree
So as not to be bitterly disappointed, accept the things you cannot change
If you can change things, do them better next time
Indeed, these are the realities of life

The Realities of Life | Lorna Ramirez

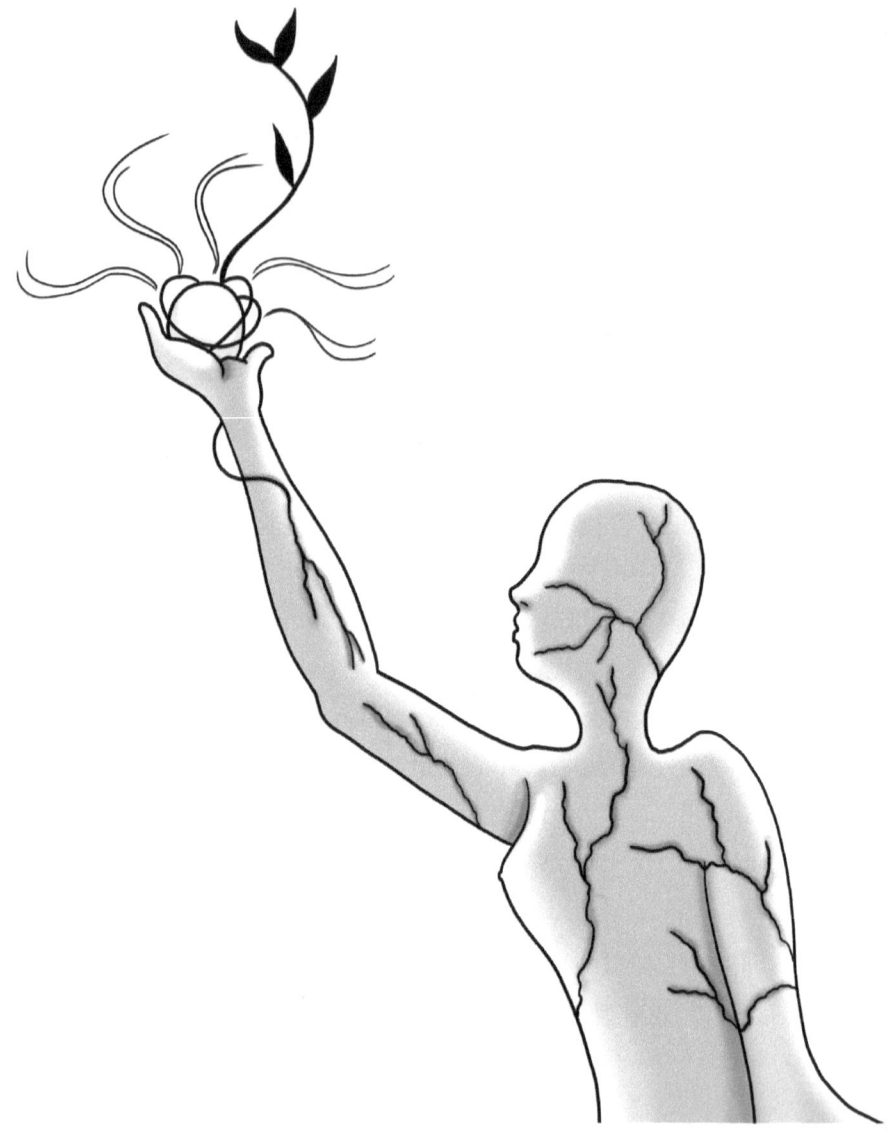

2. SUFFERING IN SILENCE

At times we cry within
Yet no one can hear
The pain and hurt, only you can feel
Those shattered dreams and memories of yester-years that
haunt you vividly as only they can
But that was then and today is different
Years have passed and things have changed
Once again, triumphantly, you emerge now
A better, stronger person

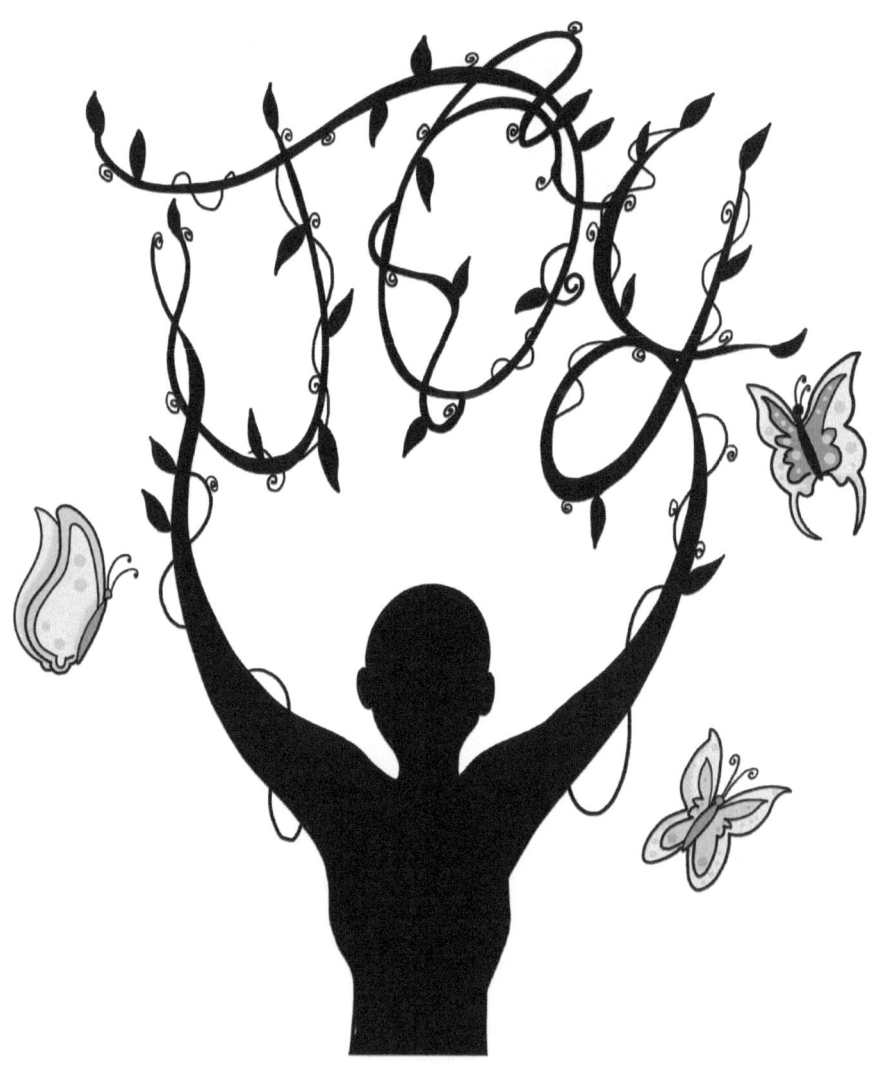

3. LOVING YOUR LIFE

Love the life you live
Appreciate the things you have
Be it small or big, wake up each day with enthusiasm
Full of hope and determination that today will be
Better than yesterday
Make tomorrow another day of joy and bliss

4. OUR GIFT TO MANKIND

It is with giving that we find the joy of sharing
It is in loving that we can fully feel how it is to be loved
It is in understanding that we can practise the art of compassion
It is by believing in ourselves that we can focus and do
anything our hearts desire
And most importantly
It is in trusting and believing in Him
That we can find all the inspiration and courage to do these things

The Realities of Life | Lorna Ramirez

5. A MOTHER'S LOVE

Giving without expecting in return
Loving with all thy heart no matter what
Understanding when others fail to understand
Supporting in times of sorrow and grief
Most of all,
Always being there for thy children in every way

The Realities of Life | Lorna Ramirez

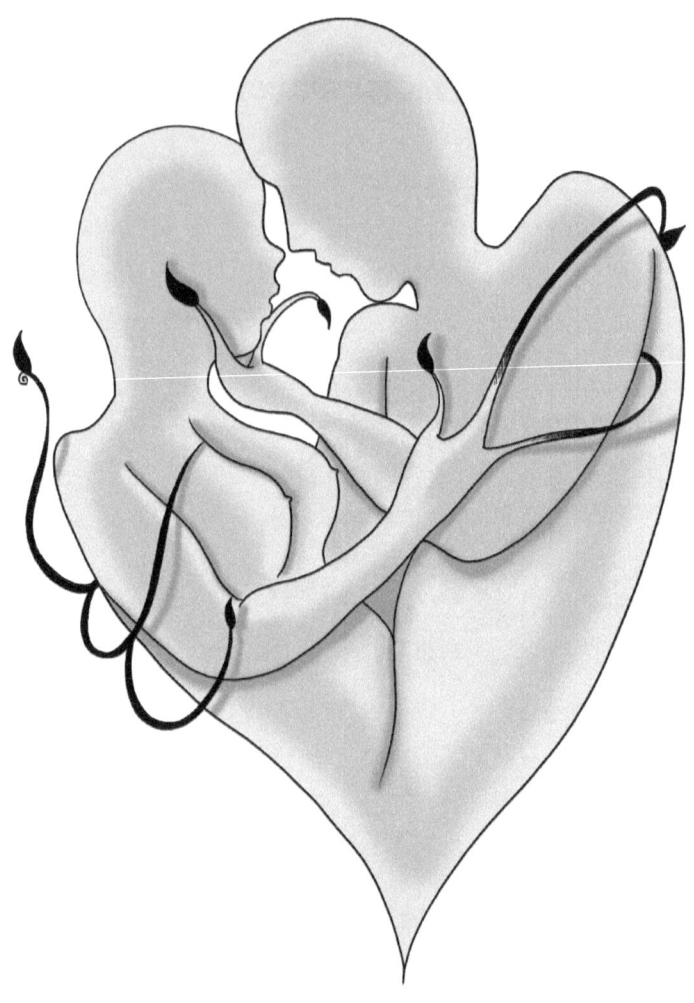

6. DEDICATED TO ALL HUSBANDS

He may not have the same thick curly hair
He may not have the lean physique
He may not have the same smooth baby-face look
But there are things that remain unchanged
He still has that cheeky smile
Same facial expression when angry, sad or happy
Still has the same sense of humour
Through the years he has always been
My mentor, my rock, my guide, my fiercest critic
But most of all, my real best friend
Like others, we have our highs and lows
But because of our love and support for each other We have
managed to go through each trial and triumph
If given the chance to do it over again
Without hesitation, I would do so,
With no regrets

7. NEVER

Never lose hope without fighting
Never give up without even trying
Never stop loving; it's the reason for living
Never stop believing in yourself
It's the secret of success
Never stop trusting Him
He will always know what is best for us

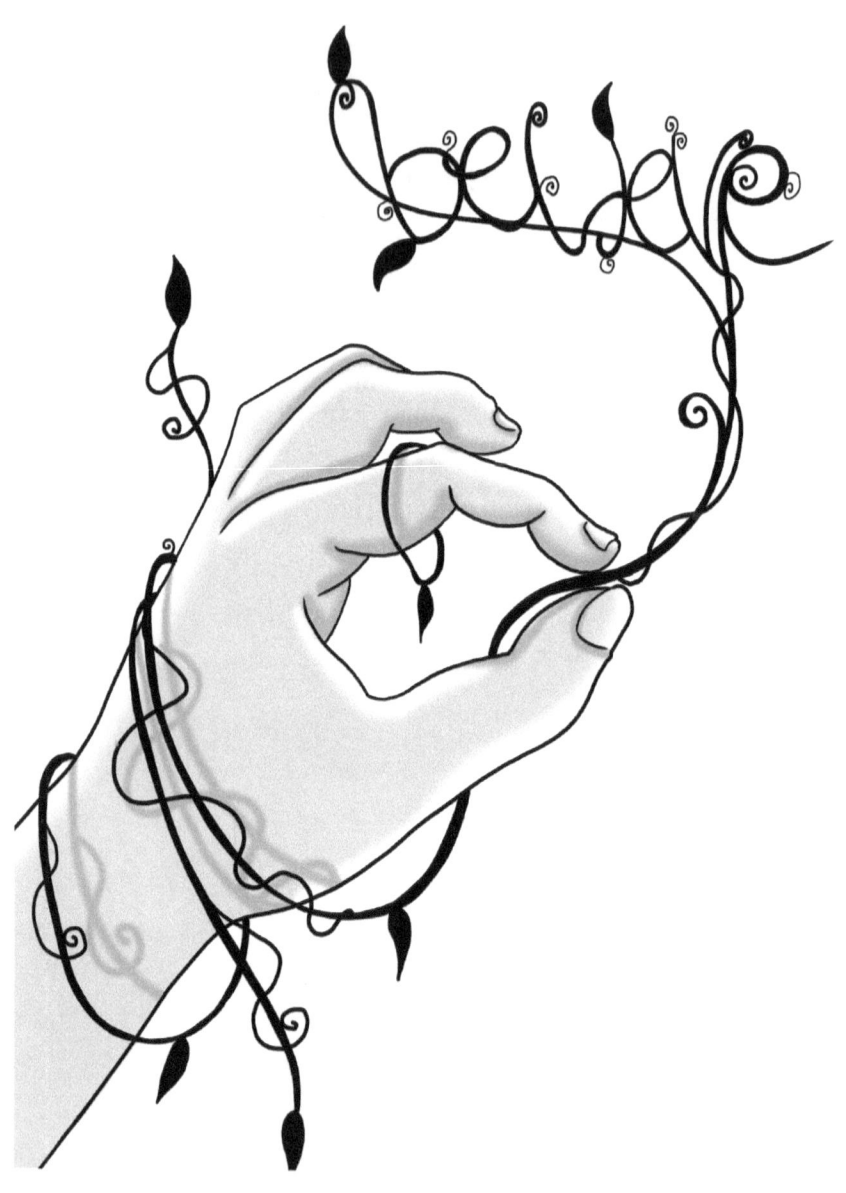

8. IT DOES NOT MATTER

It does not matter what they say
It does not matter what they think of you
It does not matter how they judge you
What matters most is being happy
Happy for the things you do
And believing in yourself

9. PRAISE THY LORD

Thank thee, Oh Lord
For all the wisdom
Bestowed upon me
For all the thoughts and words
That inspire me to write
If this is just a tool and way
For me to reach others
Console those who need the most
I am happy to do so
I know you will always be here
In my heart, mind and soul

10. PERSEVERANCE

In times of troubles
We sometimes question
Our very own existence
In times of mourning
We can find solace
In the arms of our loved ones
The past can be forgotten
But there are moments
The memories still haunt us
No matter how painful it was
We have to accept things as they are
Learn to move on
Tomorrow will be another day
Another day, hopefully
Of happiness and contentment

The Realities of Life | Lorna Ramirez

11. NEVER STOP

Never stop learning
Never stop stimulating your brain
Never stop believing in yourself
Never stop following your dreams
Never stop doing things
You are passionate about
Continually challenge yourself
Setting up goals to be an achiever
After all, life is too short
To be wasting your precious time

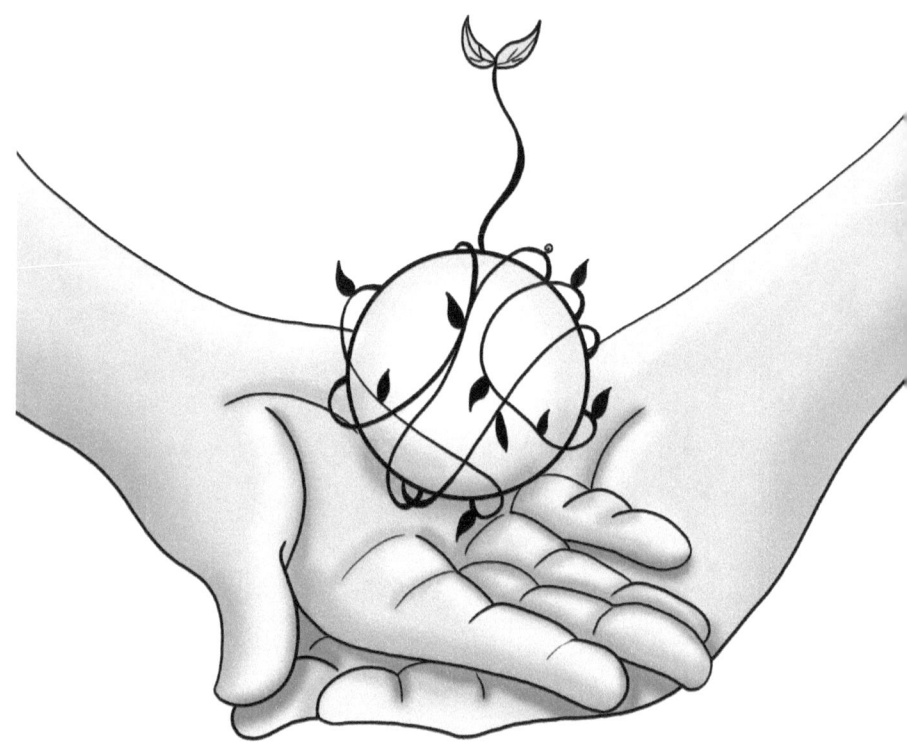

12. SPECIAL MOMENTS

Each special moment
Has that special meaning
That will be forever
Embedded in our hearts
Each challenge and endeavour
We have gone through
Needs patience, hope and perseverance
From each failure and mistake we have made
Lessons can be learned
Can be used as an inspiration
To start all over again
Till we have achieved our dreams.

13. GRANDCHILDREN

Grandchildren are sheer joy to have
Rekindled fun memories
Of the kids we once had
They bring happiness to the next phase of our lives
Now that we are in
The twilight years of our lives
We cannot get enough of them
All those special moments shared
It brings back our youth
The energy, zest and vigour we once had
And we thought we had lost

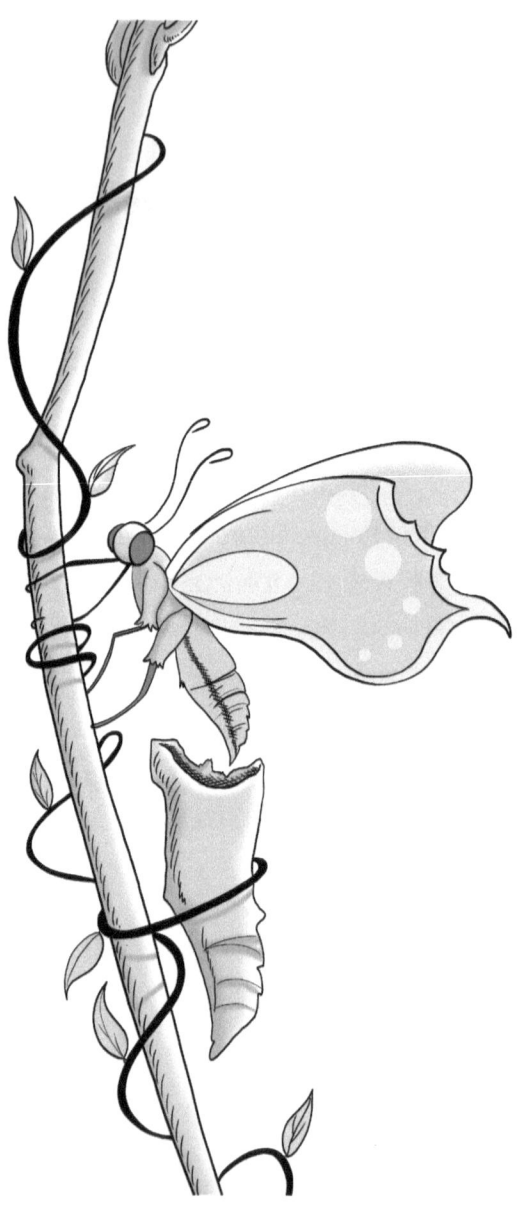

14. CHANGE

Change means courage, discipline
Change means humility
Acceptance of your fault and inadequacies
Change means enlightenment
The truth revealed
Change means aspiring
To do the right things at the right time
Take one step at a time.
With sheer determination
You can be a better person
Than you are now

The Realities of Life | Lorna Ramirez

15. LOVE (ACCEPTANCE)

It's easy to love the lovable
It's easy to accept people
Who share our beliefs and convictions
It's easy to love families and friends
It will take courage for us
To love and accept people
Who are different, unlovable
This world would be a peaceful place
If we tried to accept and respect everyone
Regardless of gender, race or religion
And other differences

The Realities of Life | Lorna Ramirez

16. MY FAITH IN GOD

With every quest I went through
With every trial I endured
With every frustration I had
With every fall I suffered
Without a doubt in my mind
I was able to go through all these
Because I knew that all these times
God would guide me and help me
Find the right way
And the right path to cross

My Inner Thoughts

1. I BELIEVE

Whenever there is Hope, inner strength will follow
Whenever there is Love, compassion will prevail
Whenever there is Struggle, solutions will be near and it will finally come to an end
Whenever there is Doubt, one day you will find the light
These are only a few of the many things that will cross our paths
And our strong belief and trust in Him will help us overcome
All the difficulties we can encounter at any time in our lives

2. THANKSGIVING

Never a day passes that I don't thank Him for all the blessings
I have
For the moment I wake up each day pain-free and still full
of energy
Able to do things that I am passionate about
Being grateful and feeling blessed having such a caring,
wonderful family, relations and friends
When the time comes, I will be able to face Him proudly and
I will be able to say
Though I have not amassed great fortune and fame
I have done my part well as a mother, wife and friend
At peace with everybody
And always connected to Thee

3. ANGER

There are times we can equate Anger to Pain
Some are angry because they feel the pain of being abused,
neglected, frustrated and betrayed
Whatever the reasons may be
One should always be strong and use the anger to fight back
and overcome
Be focused to succeed and conquer the pain you feel

4. SPIRITUAL UPLIFTMENT

If the food we take nourishes our body
Prayers, meditations and contemplations are the tools
enriching and uplifting our spiritual souls
Through these we grow to control our minds and emotions
Thus bringing us to the next level where inner peace and
satisfaction can easily be achieved

5. NEVER STOP

Once you stop dreaming
Once you stop doing things you are passionate about
Stop making goals and stop being focused
You stop living
These are our inspirations and motivations
To wake up each day
Embrace the present with open arms and with the anticipation
That you will make the day better than yesterday
And tomorrow will be another day of challenge

6. THE PRICE OF FAME

At times a person is consumed by their success
They start to detach themselves with the real world
Even neglecting their loved ones and friends
It's sad; a high price to pay for fame

7.

All of us have gone through several stages in life
Each stage is a learning experience
At the end it's nice to look back
Not counting the years you have gone through
But counting the special moments
That you had been through

8.

Open your heart to those who need the most
Help and comfort to those who are grieving, confused
and disillusioned
At times like this they needed someone to cling to
Your support can at least ease the burden that they are carrying
At times like this, friendship will be put to the test
Lucky are those who have faithful friends and loving families
To support them in their darkest moments in life

9.

Take control of your life
You have the choice to be miserable or to be happy
To be successful or be a failure
And most of all
A choice to be a good and righteous person
Or a person of deceit and evil

10.

Isn't it surprising you think you know a person because
of the years you have known them?
But you are wrong; they are not what you thought they were

11.

Why would I want all the wealth in the world?
Why would I want all the fame and glory
Where I don't know who are my real friends and enemies?
Yes, it's true
There are those who have both fame and glory
Yet, they don't have peace within themselves
Out of desperation, their only way is to drown in drugs and alcohol
And then find they are more confused
That will lead them to self-destruction and even death
I don't envy them
As long as I have enough to live, surrounded with people I trust
and love
I feel I am the luckiest person on Earth

12.

Friends that last forever and loving families
These are priceless, worth more than the riches in the world
They give us the reasons that life is worth living

13.

At times to be hurt is needed
To remind us that we are not as invincible as we perceived
we were
Disappointments are at times essential
To awaken us to the realities of life
That not everything is always within our reach
Failures can at times act as a catalyst for us to strive more
And can be a tool to open the door for success

14.

Don't fret about your previous mistakes
Be focused on the present
Concentrate on your strongest point
Thus in time, you will reach the pinnacle of success

15.

Nothing is permanent: people, places, surroundings change
At times for better or for worse
Though at times we resist changes
It is inevitable; it will happen one day
To avoid frustrations, disappointments and expectations, one must always be flexible and be prepared for when it happens

16.

Even though it took us numerous years to realise and open our eyes to the stupid things we did
Change is always worth it and necessary irrespective of our age
This is in order to make the remaining years of life memorable and enjoyable

17.

Fear of the unknown is one of the reasons we are reluctant to
do the things out of our comfort zone
But once we have decided to take the risk and have
succeeded, the benefits are endless
Then, we will never look back
For those of us who have failed
At least we can learn from our mistakes
Thus inspiring us to do it better next time around

18.

We sometimes wish that things would be different from the present
However, just counting our blessings and the things we are enjoying now
Will ease our disappointments and frustrations
Accept that in life
We cannot have everything we wish for

19.

Our kids are the reflections of us
If we give them love, support, inspire them to do things they like
For sure they will do the same for their own kids – just a cycle of life.

20.

Never cease loving, caring, believing and being positive
These are what life is all about
They are the reasons that make our journey in life easier,
meaningful and inspirational

21.

We should never pass the day without thanks for our blessings
Each day is a challenge we have to face
Each day is another day on which we will be able to build our dreams and foundations for a better tomorrow
Don't let it be wasted

22.

Yes, we are humbled by our own experience
A great person will hold his head up high
Regardless of the outcome
And graciously accept the defeat
As long as you do your best, it's all that matters
Of course, people can sometimes be cruel
Criticising and insulting and making fun of you – an ugly side to human behaviour
However after the fall
You must do some soul-searching
And start to question yourself about your priorities in life

23.

We should always know our own limitations or know when to stop
At times we are so immersed in our fame, success and glory
That we think we are invincible or indestructible
Soon we realise that we are not

24.

Each of us has a cross to carry
Each of us will go through trying times in our lives
But with our faith, our trust in Him
And with the support of families and friends
The crosses will be bearable
To carry throughout our journey in life

25.

I could feel the pain of the parents
Worrying about their kids' futures
Despite our very good intentions
To guide our kids, the correct path to follow
We must remember
That the influence of the environment, friends
Is stronger than the love we have for them
Today's culture is so different from when we were young
Nothing much we can do but to let them
Know that we are always there for them
Regardless
Such a tough role to be a parent

26.

There are the moments
That are precious
That we tend to relive and remember
Each time, it makes us happy and puts a
smile on our faces
But there are memories that should be
forgotten and instead serve as a lesson
learned in our lives

27.

It is in the realm of one's experiences
That we learn to know
What is right or wrong
What is ethical or not
But some are just too stubborn
To accept their past mistakes
Relentlessly doing the same mistakes
Over and over again

28.

Regardless of the pain we feel
From the loss of our loved ones
We, the living, should be strong
Continue to move on for the sake
Of the living loved ones
We still have

29.

Test of the real character of a person is
shown
By how they react or respond
To every unexpected event or situation
That confronts them

30.

Giving does not mean expecting
To receive in return
Loving does not mean
Changing the person for your own self intent
Believing does not mean being blinded
And shielded from facing the truth
Hoping does not mean not realising your
Own limitations and inadequacies

31.

Love is given freely
The takers should not take it for granted
Instead it should be cherished, nurtured
And protected
Once it disappears, you will be missing
The most important thing in your life

32.

At times we are so much concerned
On wanting so many things in our lives
Thus, taking too much clutter within
That we fail to identify and prioritise
The most important thing in our lives

33.

When blessings and good fortune
Come in abundance
We tend to take these for granted
But soon realise the loss
Once these are taken away from us

34.

We try as much as we can
To hold on to something
No matter how precious it is
There will come a time
To have to let it go and move on

35. I BELIEVE

That life does not need to be perfect
Imperfection challenges, motivates,
stimulates
The desire to grow and be a better person
Imperfection makes us humble
Helps us to accept
Things we cannot change
Imperfection enables us to see life
From a different perspective
Perhaps so we can see more in-depth meaning
To what life is all about

36.

It's not about making it to the top
Being successful and famous, in your career
It's all about giving back
Generously to the community
Some of your time
Specially to those needing the most

37.

Demons, monsters, evil are very true
Yet we cannot see them
Because they are lurking within ourselves
Fight and conquer them we must
For if we fail
Eventually they will poison and overtake
Our body, mind and soul

38. SUCCESS

A word which equates to hard work, perseverance and determination
Sadly, at times
These are not a guarantee or recipe for success.
Though, however hurtful it may be
We have to accept things as they are Changing your focus and directions will help
Possibly this time the road to success will be on your side

39. I BELIEVE

Prayers are not the only way to talk, to communicate with God. There are other ways such as simple acts of kindness to others. I am close with nature while working in the garden. I can show my appreciation of all the beautiful creations He had given us. I am a good mother, grandmother, friend and respect for others.

I can show Him I am following one of the commandments 'Love thy neighbour' and I strongly believe what matters most is following all that He preaches. These are more potent ways of expressing your love for Him.

40.

Who said miracles do not exist anymore?
From the moment I open my eyes each morning
I see the sun shining in the sky
Or hear the sound of the rain
Pouring down on my roof
I see life in it.
Beautiful creations from God
Enjoying the sun
Feasting from the pouring rain, the crops that we planted
bearing its fruit
I see miracles in these
Indeed, about the harmonious relationship of nature and
mankind
A simple thing I can say is
'Miracle of life'

41.

Loving someone has its negative side
You feel the pain when you see them hurting
You worry and pray that nothing bad will happen to them.
You wish and hope that they will be able to cope with the challenges along the way
However I will say
These are only a small price to pay for the blessings, blissful happiness and joy of having someone to love
And in turn to be loved

42. EVERYTHING CHANGES

People, places, things surrounding us
We change through the years
Physically, emotionally, mentally and spiritually
Loving someone means continually
Accepting them, what they are today
Rather than what they were yesterday

43.

While 'love, understanding, compassion' are
The foundations of all Goodness in the world
'Hatred, greed, hunger for power' are the very reasons
Evil exists here on earth

44.

Being happy doesn't need to be expensive
Happiest I am, in my backyard admiring my flowers, trees, plants
Happiest I am each time I tickle the ivory keys playing my
favourite piece
There are wonders in life that make people happy
That money can't buy

45.

With my strong faith in 'Him'
Plus the love and support of
My families, friends I know
I can get through all the
Challenges I face
As I walk through the journey of life.

46. LETTING IT GO

Does not mean forgetting the past
It is merely a preparation
For the new beginning
New life, new hope
Use your past as an inspiration
For a better future

47.

After grieving, the healing process
Is a long road to tackle
With your strong faith in Him
Positive attitude in life
You can do it in time

48.

Death will always leave
A gaping hole in our heart
It will take time to heal
But all the beautiful memories
Will always be treasured and kept
In our hearts

49.

It is very frustrating
When your best intentions
Are often misunderstood
And misinterpreted in
A negative way
But then again we
Have to realise that
We cannot please everybody, every time

50.

I still believe that all of us
Regardless of who and what we are
Still have a soft spot and have
Some kindness in our hearts

51.

It is what we reveal of ourselves
That could give others the wrong impression
That makes us vulnerable
To different kinds of deceit
Thus having advantage taken
Of our generosity and good intentions

52.

An act of kindness
Done wholeheartedly
Can go a long way
More than you realise
One way we can all
Make a difference

53.

Quite a few times
You thought you knew a person well
But really you don't

54. I BELIEVE

One of the many ways to achieve peace within
Is not to compare yourself with others
But learn to accept and be
Who you are and the best of
What you are

55.

My great admiration is for the people who
In spite of all the adversities, heartaches and
tribulations they have gone through
Manage to stand on their own two feet
Are successful in life
And also help others

56.

Most of us love to dwell on the past
We should let it go and move on
What matters is the present
The past is only memories
That will inspire us not to make
The same mistakes, but strengthen us
To aspire to be better and stronger

57.

In our younger days, we were so eager
To learn new things, venture into new experiences
Enjoy each time we went through
Extensive knowledge we so desired
But it is in our mature years we can
Comprehend, understand and appreciate
Appreciate everything we have learned and experienced
through the years

58.

As much as we love, cherish
Adore our grandkids
We must keep in mind
That they are not ours
The parents have the last say
In any decision or in any
Other future circumstances

59.

What's the best thing about being retired?
First and foremost, there is no pressure of work
You don't have to prove yourself each time
It's a chance to discover oneself and develop new interest in life
You have the time to look after grandkids and the best of all
No Monday blues, every day is a holiday
We worked hard before and
We all deserve a happy and joyous retirement

60.

We don't expect to live forever
So make each day a Celebration of Life
Each day thanking Him for
All the graces we do have
Savour each precious moment
You spend with loved ones, families and friends
If you fail to do so
One day you will realise
You missed the most important
Things in your life
That money couldn't buy.

61.

Others hide their sorrows through their smiles
Others hide their fears by acting fearlessly
Others hide their insecurity by being boastful all the time
Others hide their inferiority by acting superior to everyone
At times the things that we see are not really what they are
There more depths and meanings to consider before judging others

62. I BELIEVE

True friendship does not take a day to make
Just like Rome was not built in a day
It takes fine wine years to age and to attain perfection
Friendship takes years to develop
Those memories good ones and bad ones
You share together
Accepting of one's faults and inadequacies
Understanding and forgiveness
And if the time comes when you won't see each other again
Beautiful memories of friendship
That no one can take away from you
Will remain embedded in your heart

63. I BELIEVE

Quality of life and success of a person
Cannot be measured
By being rich
Nor by being famous
It can only be measured
If you have inner peace
A loving family
And real friends who always care for you

64.

Children laughing and playing
Hugs and kisses of your grandkids, kids
The beautiful aroma of your wife's cooking
The sight of the magnificent flowers, plants blossoming
Sometimes the best things in life to be enjoyed
Are just
The simplest things in life

65.

Waking up each day without expecting anything
Always thanking each day for my blessings enjoyed
Savouring each minute, moment, of what life has to offer
Enjoying to the fullest the beautiful surroundings
The beautiful people such as loved ones and friends
Whom have given me joy and made my journey in life
So interesting and meaningful
And most of all
Had a part of making me what I am today

66. SUCCESS IS

How quickly you get up
Each time you fall
And never lose hope

67. ON RETIREMENT

I was often asked these questions
Are you bored being retired?
How do you fill up your time?
I just smile
I don't have to explain anything
Because I know within
I am enjoying every minute of being retired
How can you be bored sharing precious moments with
your loved ones?
How can you be bored when you can explore and
re-invent yourself?
How can you be bored when now you can do things you are passionate about?
How can you be bored if you keep challenging yourself and stimulating your brain
At times I wish there were twenty-eight hours in a day
To fill up my very busy life

68. CALAMITY

How easy it is to unmake years of hard work, sacrifices,
time and effort
To watch them disappear in seconds
These are the feelings of the people affected by disasters
and calamities
Really a tough word we live in
The very reason why we should acknowledge each day
as a blessing
Each day as a challenge

My Wisdoms

1.

Live in this world not as people expect you to be but as you really want to be.
One element towards achieving happiness in life

2.

Never fear to take risks and be out of your comfort zone
It is the only way to find your ultimate strength and capabilities
That at times you are not even aware of

3.

It takes courage to forgive
But it takes twice the courage to ask for forgiveness

4.

Expect the unexpected
Expect the inevitable
Change the things within your grip, but don't despair For the things you can't change – that's how life is

5.

Evil disguises itself in many forms
It is up to us to {whether we } fall to {into} its treacherous trap

6.

Intricate and complexity of human emotions and minds are
difficult to comprehend
At times you think you know a person well
But soon realise you don't

7.

One of the reasons why some people are miserable and discontented in their lives
Is because they are always comparing themselves with others
Instead of just being themselves

8.

With so many things kept cluttered in our hearts
We fail to find a space for Him to reside in our hearts
The sign of modern times

9.

Don't waste your time regretting your past mistakes
Or you will live forever miserably
You are then unable to look forward to brighter days in your life

10.

The only way to be non-judgemental is to accept people
for what they are
Be it a difference of religion, culture belief or value
Each one of us can start by
Thus making this world an ideal place to live

11.

There are times when what you perceive about yourself
Is not necessarily the same
As what others think of you

12.

It does not matter how old you are, provided you know your own limitations
You can still follow your dream and work for it
You will be surprised by what you can achieve

13.

One of the many things I have learned from life
It is far better to not expect anything and be surprised
Than to be bitterly disappointed over something you were expecting to happen

14.

Words are so powerful
They are like a sword
They can pierce you right through your heart

15.

It's not about what you have and
It's not about when you made it to the top
It's all about being passionate and happy with what you do
It's also all about being at peace with yourself, others and God

16.

Quite often many words are left unspoken,
Either too hurtful or too intense
These words would not be enough to express it

17.

At times we get hurt by the very people we trusted
But then again, being unable to trust anyone can make our lives miserable

18.

A person who pretends too much will at the end be confused about the difference between reality and fantasy

19.

Always be what you are and let people
Accept you for who you are and not what they think you are

20.

One day you will realise the things you take for granted
are as precious as gold

21.

You learn hundred times more from life's experiences than you learn in the classroom

22.

Being a parent you learn to love unconditionally
By making self-sacrifices as a parent you become more sensitive to all the issues around
Wishing one day your kids will learn how to tackle and survive in this tough world

23.

Just live for today
What is important is the present
Yesterday is just a memory, where the good is to be treasured
and the bad should be forgotten
Make another day of hope and blissful living

24.

When we stop doing the things we are passionate about
That's the time we stop living

25.

We criticise others
Based on what we perceive
To be right or wrong

26.

When the tears dry up and stop flowing
That's the time you can
Feel the intensity of your pain

27.

You have done your best
And your best is still not good enough
Don't despair
It's probably not meant to happen
Luck and destiny are in full control

28.

Believing and dreaming is one thing
Taking actions on what you believe is another thing
Just believing and having the passion are the best weapons for success

29.

Experiences in life
Enrich one's knowledge
Always the best mentors
In your life

30.

When one becomes overwhelmed and cannot speak
It's best to keep silent
Then the silence becomes more powerful than words

31.

Living in the past will only cause
Heartaches and frustrations
Deter us from moving forward

32.

It's love that makes us do the impossible
Can't be seen, but can be felt
It's so powerful
It can turn a person into a beast
Or a beast into an angel

33.

It's not about life
It's all about
How you live your life

34.

Fear not Death
It's only the beginning
Of a new life

35.

Truth hurts
But no matter how hurtful it is
It is an effective way
To bring a change

36.

Music can connect people
Can bring them together
Regardless of religion, gender and belief

37.

It is what we make our life
That makes life itself
Full of challenges and surprises

38.

It's easier to love than to hate
But some people do it
The other way around

39.

Hope always bring comfort
Strength to each endeavour

40.

Greed, hungry for power are akin to drugs
So addictive once tasted
You don't know how
And when to stop

41.

Some people would quit
Without even trying
One way of missing out

42.

At times in some circumstances
You have to please first yourself before others

43.

Such a beautiful gesture of friendship
They are always there to help you
In time of your needs
Support you when needed
Guide and lead you

44.

Challenging yourself
Insatiable quest
For perfection and knowledge
These are effective tools
To be successful in life

45.

At times we need a big fall and disappointment
To awaken us to our senses
To know that we are not invulnerable
As we thought we were
Restores the goodness within which we once had.

46.

At times we are more concerned
With what others would say or think
Thus affecting our judgement
To act in the right and sensible way

47.

A life fully treasured
Fully enjoyed
Is worth all the richness
In the world
Priceless

48.

At times you will be surprised
That a stranger you met before
Can one day help you
In time of need

49.

Yesterday's lessons and
Soul-searching experiences
Are needed to make the
Present foundation effective
And stronger for a better
And successful tomorrow

50.

It is what you believe
Convictions, principles in life
That will lead you
to what you are today

51.

We sometimes falter and fail
But what matters most
Is how quickly we stand up
And have the courage to
Do it all over again
Till we have succeeded and attained
What we were aiming for

52.

There are things in life
That we perceive
Are not what they really are
And sometimes even the smartest person
Can be deceiving, often times
Evil can hide and pose in the shadow of goodness

53.

Old friends are worth keeping
But there will also be a room for new ones
You never know
You can still find new ones worth keeping

54.

It's not about the quantity or length of time you spent on earth
It's all about the quality of life you make for yourself and others

55.

At times the things that
We see are only illusions
You have to dig deeper
Analyse, understand
What really lies beneath the surface

56.

I want to be accepted as I am
Not how others want me to be

57.

When in doubt and confused
Listen to your heart
It will take you there {to where you should be}

58.

Don't let frustrations, disappointments overtake you
Instead, make them your friends
Strive more and aim higher
Till the pinnacle of success is achieved

59.

Dreams are only the start
Taking action is the ultimate beginning
To make your dreams come true

60.

There's nothing more glorious
Than to hear and see
The laughter and sound
Of happy kids
Playing in my house

61.

Each day you wake up
Is already a blessing
Regardless of what you do
Make each day as special as can be

62.

Denial is the deadliest hindrance
To making a change and moving forward

63.

You cannot achieve
Inner peace
Unless
Envy and hatred
No longer
Reign in your heart

64.

You cannot run forever
For all your problems and fear
Will catch you unexpectedly one day
With dire consequences

65.

It's not about the quantity of time
That you spend with your loved ones
It's all about the quality
How you spend the time with them
That's what matters most

66.

Hope is the only thing we try to hold on
Amidst our frustrations
Disappointments and sorrows
Without it we could not move on
And have the courage to face what lies ahead

67.

Grandkids
What priceless gifts
Given to us by our own kids
Won't trade them for anything in the world

68.

Lots of things in our lives are so simple
We make it so complicated
Hence at the end we are trapped
With our own wrongdoing

69.

A beautiful smile can melt anyone's heart
Especially the smiles from your loved ones

Also by Lorna Ramirez

Lorna Ramirez wrote this book so she could share her wisdoms with others. She has been an observer of human behaviour and emotions and has built up her own personal philosophies throughout her life. This book is a collection of her strong beliefs and convictions and offers encouragement and enlightenment to others who may be lost and confused or be looking for some positive advice and assistance. Lorna Ramirez is a woman of strong beliefs in her faith and advocates believing in oneself, perseverance when times are difficult and living in the present.

These original poems and wise sayings will be enjoyed by readers young and old, from any walks of life, for their simplicity and beauty.

This authentic story about a Filipino migrant family settling in Melbourne in 1977 is a fascinating read, as it tells of the emotions, the ups and downs, the government assistance in those days, the practicalities, the difficulties, the sudden change of lifestyle and culture but also the joys of living in Australia in the 1970s, a 'paradise' in so many ways, with great opportunities for a good life.

The wife suddenly is confronted with severe trauma, closely followed by another, a time in their lives when everything appeared perfect. Her near death experience results in new beliefs and understanding and inspires her to write.

About the Author

Lorna Ramirez was born, raised and educated in Manila in the Philippines, attaining a degree in chemical engineering and working as a laboratory manager in a textiles company.

In 1977, with her husband and her son and daughter, she migrated to Australia. She worked as a laboratory technician and a chemist in Australia, only retiring in the year 2000 to care for her first grandchild.

Lorna Ramirez has travelled extensively, gaining much from her interactions with people all over the world and building a strong foundation for her philosophies about life. She loves gardening, cooking and reading and playing the piano. She is also interested in the stock exchange.

She has published two books: My Innermost Thoughts in 2014 and My Passion, My Calling in 2015. In October 2016 Lorna was one of the recipients of a certificate of recognition from FILCCA (Filipino Community Council of Australia).

Lorna is also a regular contributor for The Philippine Times in Melbourne and The Philippine Sentinel in Sydney.

www.ingramcontent.com/pod-product-compliance
Lightning Source LLC
Chambersburg PA
CBHW032038290426
44110CB00012B/863